W9-BYE-943

How to Talk to Your

DOG

How to Talk to Your

DOG

Jean Craighead George

Illustrated by Sue Truesdell

HarperCollinsPublishers

Photographs of Jean Craighead George by Addie Passen

Library of Congress Cataloging-in-Publication Data

George, Jean Craighead, date

   How to talk to your dog / Jean Craighead George ; illustrated by Sue Truesdell.

      p.   cm.

   Summary: Describes how dogs communicate with people through their behavior and sounds
and explains how to talk back to them using sounds, behavior, and body language.

   ISBN 0-06-027092-6. — ISBN 0-06-027093-4 (lib. bdg.)

   1. Dogs—Behavior—Juvenile literature.   2. Human-animal communication—Juvenile literature.
[1. Dogs.   2. Human-animal communication.   3. Pets.]   I. Truesdell, Sue, ill.   II. Title.

SF426.5.G46   2000   98-41515

636.70887—dc21   CIP

                                                   AC

3 4 5 6 7 8 9 10   ❖

To Qimmiq,
my wonderful talking dog
—J.C.G.

For Buddy
—S.T.

No one

will ever love you

as much as your dog does.

He will follow you devotedly.

He will accept your scoldings

and still think you're wonderful.

He will do your every bidding.

He will sit, heel, stay,

and come when you call.

He will sleep by your bed,

defend you from enemies,

and be your friend

until he dies.

How did this wonderful state of affairs come to be?

Dogs are descended from wolves. Most do not not look like wolves anymore, but they still have their best traits. They are friendly. They adore their leader—you—and they talk to other dogs and to you in their own tongue.

What is this dog talk?

It is sound: whimpers, growls, sniffs, barks, and howls. It is visual: tail wags, ear twists, eye movements, and other body language. It is chemical: odors and taste. It is physical contact: the touch of a friend or the whack of an enemy.

Speak to your dog in his own language. He will reward you by being an even more devoted friend.

Dog talk should begin as early as possible.

Seven or eight weeks is the best age to take a pup home. He will replace his love for his mother with love for you. Do as she did: Feed him, pick him up, hug him, pet him, and whimper into his fur. That's mother-dog talk.

Say his name often. You will know when he recognizes it. He will turn and look at you, and his eyes will brighten.

Praise him. Tell him what a good dog he is. Dogs love flattery. Flattery will put him in a good mood, and it will be easier to teach him to sit, stay, heel, and come. Reward his achievements with treats and praise. Treats and saying, "Good dog," are gold stars for puppies. Eventually, praise will be enough.

No matter how old your dog is, you can speak to him in his own language at any time in his life. "Hello" is a good way to begin. Dogs greet each other by sniffing noses.

To say hello to your dog, sniff toward his nose. That's dog talk. He will answer by pulling his ears back and close to his head. What he is saying is "Hello, leader."

There is also the joyous hello. When you return home, your dog greets you bounding, tail wagging, body swishing, and with his head lowered in deference to you. He might lick you to seal the welcome. You don't have to lick back. That would please him, but he will love you even if you don't. A hug or head pat is your "joyous hello" to your dog.

"Good night" in dog talk is physical.

Rub your dog's head, ears, and neck. Lower your lids and sigh into his fur. You are the mother dog licking her pup off to sleep.

"Good-bye" is a whisk of the tail, then turning and walking off. Since you don't have a tail, swish your hand downward and show your back. If your dog does not choose to hear this unwelcome message and races after you, tell him, "I am boss," in dog talk, then repeat the dog "good-bye."

5

How do you say, "I am boss"?

The most effective way is to put your mouth on his muzzle. That means in dog talk that you are the leader. His ears will go back and against his head, and his tail will lower. This is his way of saying, "Yes, you are my leader."

If you don't want to use your mouth, take his muzzle in your hand and gently shake it as you say, "Good dog." Telling your dog he is good is his reward for living. Finally, give the dog good-bye and walk off. He should let you go.

If he comes running after you, don't get mad at him. Hug him and tell him he's good, and repeat the conversation. You should never leave your dog with a scolding.

One thing you should know when your dog is still young is that dogs, even puppies, want to be boss. When dog meets dog, one dominates the other by lifting his head higher. He will put his paw on a shoulder of the other to clinch his message. Your dog will try to dominate you by jumping up. Don't let him. Go to the "I am boss" talk and repeat it several times. A deep voice is also "boss." Keep your voice low when you speak to him.

Then hold your head high, your chest out. That posture says to your dog, "I am a leader." This is body language. Kings, queens, presidents, and military leaders speak of their high rank with this same posture.

Keep telling your dog you're in charge. His love for you, the leader, will deepen.

"I am your humble servant" is a posture. Wolves say this by rolling onto their backs and flashing their white stomach fur just like our white flag of surrender. Dogs do the same thing, even though many breeds don't have white bellies. Lying on their backs, feet bent, is their ultimate declaration of submissiveness. You are truly in charge when your dog shows you his belly.

Some kids roll onto their backs when they are playing with their dog. Don't do it. You are telling him, "I am your humble servant." He will react to this news by jumping on you, putting his paws on your chest, lifting

his head above yours, and throwing up his ears and tail to say, "I am boss."

Change your message. Get on your feet and tell him you are boss.

Dogs love to play. They invite each other to tumble and romp by spanking their forepaws on the ground, rear ends up, tails wagging.

Get down on all fours and spank the ground with your hands and forearms to invite your friend to play. Be prepared. He will come leaping on top of you and might even knock you over. He is saying, "You bet, I want to play!"

A great deal of dog talk is a soundless language. You speak this way to your dog without your even knowing it. When you are about to leave him, your body says so. Your dog will get up and run to the door. When you are just thinking about feeding him, your movements send him romping up to you, licking his chops. He also knows when you are sick or unhappy; he will lie near you, his head on his outstretched paws, brow furrowed.

People arriving at your house tell your dog through body language whether they are an enemy or a friend. Your dog will let you know which they are. He will walk stiff-leggedly toward an enemy, ears back, tail straight out. To a friend he will lower his head as he does to you. His tail will wag. His face will be smooth and at ease. Visitors, kids, and deliverypersons evoke different poses from your dog. Relatives, on the other hand, will get the "welcome hello" even if your dog has never met them. Somehow most dogs know kin.

To know your dog's feelings, watch his tail. He uses it as a flag of feelings. He is happy and confident when his tail is up.[1] When it is close to his rump and down, he is depressed.[2] When he is feeling good, his tail is loose and down.[3] If he puts his tail up with a crick in it, he is threatening, probably another dog.[4] He is casting himself down when he brushes a lowered tail sideways.[5] He may be telling you he is sick. And he is cowed and beaten when he pulls his tail between his legs.[6]

Some dog tails are clipped, and this language is not easily read. A little study, however, will reveal that a short stump sends out quite a few messages.

Everyone knows by looking at your face if you are happy, bored, angry, or suspicious. Although your dog does not have as many facial expressions as you do, his ears, mouth, eyes, and entire face tell how he feels. When he is serene and happy, his ears are up and his head is high, his face smooth.[1] He will frown and pull back his ears when he is anxious.[2] He may squint his eyes. His angry or defensive mood is expressed in a wrinkled muzzle and exposed canine teeth.[3] A suspicious dog thrusts his head forward, presses his ears back, and frowns.[4] A wrinkled brow and ears held out to the sides say he is confused.[5]

Sniff his nose to tell him not to be angry or confused. Nose sniffs are peace talk.

1

2

3

4

5

We have such a poor sense of smell that we are left out of the most important dog talk: scent. You can get some idea of this language by watching your dog's nose. Dogs sniff in information. When they have learned all there is to know, they sneeze-snort out.

Dogs use this language to learn about their environment. When you meet a strange dog, hold out your hand and let him sniff you.

Sniff back. Your scent and sniffing tell the dog you are friendly. Although you will learn nothing by your sniffing, he will learn what sex you are and whether you're an adult or young person. He will know if you have just eaten and what it was. He will snuffle your clothes to learn more about your dog. A snuffle is more than a sniff. It is a deep inhale, a thorough investigation.

When you come home, your own dog will want to snuffle your coat and clothes. He will know where you've been and with whom. Watch his tail. If you have been with a dog he dislikes, that crick may appear, or he will whisk his tail to say he is jealous. Remind him he's the most wonderful dog in the world with a sniff or a hug.

Snuffling the crotches of people is unacceptable. The dog is saying he is invading the personal sphere of a lower-ranking individual. He is pulling rank. If your dog is guilty of this annoying habit, you may use the "threat" talk. Hold something over his head, such as a piece of folded newspaper or a glove. Anything waved above his head is disconcerting. Enemies like eagles come from above.

Dogs can tell you wonderful things by tracking with their noses. They show you where the rabbit and deer went. They can tell you a groundhog is in his hole. The gift of smell was a primary reason for domesticating the wolf. Over the eons careful breeding developed hunting specialists. Now there are bird dogs, deer dogs, badger dogs, coon dogs, and sheep dogs, to name a few.

Scent marking or urine spraying leaves chemicals that are a dog's newspaper. In it is all the neighborhood dog gossip. Through sniffs your dog knows who left the message, how he is feeling, what sex he or she is, his mood, what he's been eating, and whether he is boss or follower. The positions of your dog's tail will give you a vague

idea of what he is reading. Tail at ease is pleasant news. Tail down, the news is worrisome. When he has assimilated the messages, he will add his own news before trotting off. Females leave their newspaper on the ground when they squat-spray. They will read the male news on tree trunks and fire hydrants, but not with as much interest as the males do. Female news, however, is read avidly by male dogs.

You are limited in your ability to talk to your dog in scent, but there are a few odor messages you can give him. Get out a treat to tell him he's a good dog. He knows the odor of a treat. Rub your hands over his body and then over yours to tell him you are best friends.

One very pleasant way to talk to your dog is with your eyes. When your dog looks into your eyes with those clear brown peepers, be flattered. He is telling you that you are his friend and that he trusts you. Eye contact is bonding. It brings you and

your dog closer together. Look into his eyes whenever you can. The more you bond with him, the more he will love and obey you. In fact, you should make eye contact with him before you tell him to sit or heel or stay. He will pay more attention and learn more quickly. Look at him with kindness. Do not stare; a stare is a threat.

You can pass other messages with your eyes. Think, "I love you. I love you," and your lower lid will involuntarily come up and soften your expression. Your dog will read that and return this message by softening his eyes. Open your eyes wide when you are looking into his and he will become alert and somewhat alarmed. You are saying, "I am fearful."

You can also tell your dog "no," or that you are mad at him, with your eyes, and he will hear. People do that. How many times has your mom or dad told you to stop what you are doing with a stern look and no words at all?

Since our language is 90 percent sound, we understand the voice of the dog best of all.

Dog sounds are varied. There is the whimper and "social squeak," the sniff, the bark, the growl, and for some breeds the howl.

The whimper is an intimate sound that speaks of deep feelings. It is usually addressed to the family. It is love. It is "I want to be your friend." The eyes become brilliant, the tail wags. Whimper to your dog. He likes it.

The whimper can also be a sound of unhappiness. Dogs whose masters are harsh and overly dominant will whimper to express their insecurity.

When your dog is in a car, the soft whimper means "I know where I am." An excited whimper says, "Let's get out and walk." A slow, high whimper says he doesn't like where he's going—to the vet, to the kennel, to the house of a dog he doesn't like.

The social squeak is high and ear piercing. Much of it is out of our hearing range. It is the language between mother and pup, and is deeply bonding.

Squeak to your dog by kissing the back of your hand to produce that high note. Some dogs will howl in response, as if some primitive emotion has been stirred. Others will lick you. A lick is not a kiss. It is a statement that says you're a wonderful leader.

Growling is aggressive talk. It is unfriendly and unmistakable. Don't growl back. Dogs don't like that.

Barking is the dog talk we are most familiar with. It is an expression of excitement. A hunting dog "tongues." Some dogs have a different tongue for each different animal they are tracking. By listening, you know whether the hound is following a deer, rabbit, raccoon, or squirrel. The dog bark is usually an announcement that strangers, friends, or other animals are on your property. The bark is different for each category. Eventually you learn to know which one is coming by the intensity and variation of the bark.

Around the house your dog barks for various reasons. He barks to be fed. He barks to go out or come indoors. He will bark to ask you to take him for a walk. After a while you will realize that each bark is slightly different. The food bark is usually more sharp and demanding; the door-opening bark is lower in pitch and not so intense.

Although it is fun, it is not very rewarding to bark at your dog. He doesn't understand your bad accent and may twist his head and look at you in confusion.

Howling is the hallmark of the wolf, but some dogs can howl. To the wolf the howl serves to keep wolves in touch with each other. It is a pep rally before hunting. It also bonds the pack—and it is fun. Try howling with your classmates and see for yourself.

Some dogs howl when they hear a fire siren, a violin, or a high note that triggers their deepest instincts. Although most dogs are incapable of howling, a few individuals can learn. Howl for your dog. Enjoy your howl; make it melodic and interesting. Your dog just might lift his head, close his eyes, and howl back, tail wagging.

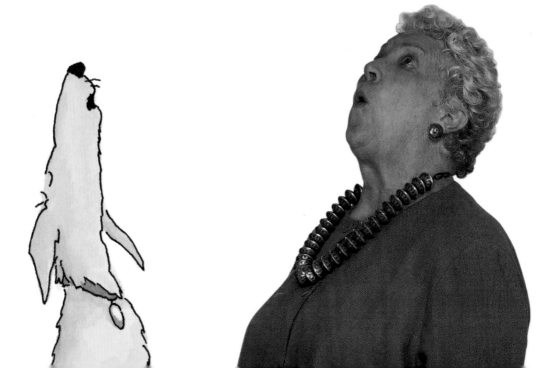

As you and your dog talk together,
you will see that dog talk is not just posture, scent,
sound, or touch alone, but shades of all braided together
into a clear and beautiful language. As the years pass,
you and your dog may even speak less and less.
You'll each know what the other wants. Your old dog
will look at you, and without a voiced command
he will sit or heel or run for the car.
You will look at your dog and take him for a walk
or toss him a Frisbee. Such are the rewards
of talk and love.

Good dog talk to you.